GIN-
DULGENCE

GIN-
DULGENCE

OVER 50 GIN COCKTAILS,
FROM ICONIC TO AVANT-GARDE

DOG 'N' BONE

Published in 2022 by Dog 'n' Bone Books
An imprint of Ryland Peters & Small Ltd

20–21 Jockey's Fields   341 E 116th St
London WC1R 4BW   New York, NY 10029

www.rylandpeters.com

10 9 8 7 6 5 4 3 2 1

A CIP catalog record for this book is available from the Library of Congress and the British Library.

ISBN: 978 1 912983 54 4

Printed in China

Recipe collection compiled by Emily Calder
For recipe and photography credits see page 64.
Illustrations by Blaire Frame.

Senior Designer Geoff Borin
Desk Editor Emily Calder
Head of Production Patricia Harrington
Production Manager Gordana Simakovic
Art Director Sally Powell
Creative Director Leslie Harrington

MIX
Paper from
responsible sources
FSC® C008047

CONTENTS

INTRODUCTION

A spirit that guarantees great vibes and good times, gin is the true star of the show when it comes to cocktails. The natural qualities of gin make it particularly good at lifting fruity flavours, and the range of gins, from flavoured, to floral to pink, make it the perfect diverse cocktail ingredient. It truly is the variety of gin-based cocktails that make it such an exciting and popular spirit, and it is a staple in classics like a Martini or the Spanish Gin Tonica. Gin can also be drunk throughout the year; ideally suited to warm summer evenings, drinks like the Raspberry Tom Collins provide the perfect refreshing lift for the warmer months of the year. More floral and subtle flavours are ideal in the springtime, with bloom-inspired hits like the Field of Dreams welcomed with open arms. The Negroni, with its orange hues, is the perfect seasonal colour match for when the leaves are falling, whilst sophisticated hits like the French 75 add suitable pizazz to winter holiday celebrations. From bartender favourites to fun new twists, you'll find all the gin-tastic inspiration you need!

WHITE LADY

The White Lady, the epitome of pale elegance, is the creation of bartender Harry McElhone, who originally made it with crème de menthe; he replaced this with gin. The egg white lends a deliciously silky glamour, but it's not essential.

25 ml/1 oz. freshly squeezed lemon juice

25 ml/1 oz. Cointreau

35 ml/1¼ oz. gin

½ egg white (optional)

Serves 2

Fill a cocktail shaker with ice cubes and add all the ingredients. Shake very well, then strain into a chilled martini glass. Serve immediately.

SAPPHIRE

GLASSWARE

Martini glass

GARNISH

Blueberries

INGREDIENTS

10 ml/2 teaspoons
Parfait Amour

50 ml/1⅔ oz. chilled gin

Serves 2

Who can resist a perfect love? Parfait Amour is a Curaçao-based, mauve-tinted liqueur infused with rose petals or violets and almonds, and it adds a seductive *je ne sais quoi* to the austerity of the very cold gin.

Make sure you chill the gin in the freezer before starting. Gently pour the Parfait Amour into a well-chilled martini glass. Pour in the gin over the rounded back of tablespoon, so that it forms a layer over the Parfait Amour. Garnish with blueberries on a cocktail stick and then serve immediately.

GIN SLING

GLASSWARE

Wine glass

GARNISH

Lemon wedge

INGREDIENTS

freshly squeezed juice
of ½ lemon

12.5 ml/⅓ oz. sugar
syrup

35 ml/1¼ oz. gin

15 ml/½ oz. cherry
brandy

soda water, to top

Serves 1

One of the earliest styles of cocktail, a sling is basically a spirit mixed with sugar and water. It has given rise to endless variations, and every bartender worth his salt would have had his own version.

Fill a cocktail shaker with ice cubes and add all the ingredients except the soda water. Shake vigorously and strain into a chilled wine glass. Top up with soda water and serve immediately.

FIELD OF DREAMS

GLASSWARE

Highball glass

GARNISH

Edible flowers

INGREDIENTS

4 mint leaves

**dash of elderflower
liqueur**

1 egg white

**20 ml/¾ oz. Kamm &
Sons Aperitif**

20 ml/¾ oz. floral gin

**60 ml/2 oz. Pea Purée
(see right)**

**10 ml/2 teaspoons
freshly squeezed
lemon juice**

Serves 1

This cocktail came about by a happy accident. It represents a field bursting with meadow flowers: the green grass is easy to replicate with the peas.

Smack the mint leaves between your palms and drop into a cocktail shaker. Add the elderflower liqueur and egg white. Cover the shaker and dry-shake hard for 20 seconds, then add the remaining ingredients and fill the shaker two-thirds of the way up with ice. Cover again and shake hard for another 20 seconds. Double-strain the mixture into a highball glass, using a tea strainer to catch any mint solids. Place your edible flowers on top of the foam and then serve immediately.

PEA PURÉE
Mix 60 g/¼ cup of fresh or thawed frozen small peas with just enough water to liquify the peas in a blender. Pulse for a few seconds, then turn up to high for 15 seconds. Strain through a fine mesh to ensure that the purée is smooth.

LA PASSEGGIATA

The passeggiata is an excellent Italian tradition of taking an evening stroll along a scenic boulevard, dressed up to the nines, to check out your neighbours. Why not give it a try down your road after breakfast, accompanied by one of these?

Half-fill a collins glass with ice cubes. Add the pink grapefruit juice, gin and Aperol and stir well. Top with prosecco and stir very briefly. If you like, squeeze a strip of grapefruit zest over the top and drop it in. Serve immediately.

MANGO MORNING

GLASSWARE

Champagne flute

GARNISH

Lemon zest

INGREDIENTS

15 ml/½ oz. gin

50 ml/1⅔ oz. mango juice

5 ml/1 teaspoon freshly squeezed lemon juice

well-chilled Cava or other sparkling wine, to top

Serves 1

This is a bright, tropical sunshine-filled alternative to the classic Mimosa or Buck's Fizz. You won't be able to help being in a good mood if you're handed one of these.

Pour the gin, mango juice and lemon juice into an ice-filled cocktail shaker and shake well. Strain into a chilled Champagne flute and top with Cava. Garnish with lemon zest, if you like, and serve immediately.

FRENCH 75

GLASSWARE

Champagne flute

GARNISH

Lemon zest

INGREDIENTS

25 ml/1 oz. gin

10 ml/2 teaspoons
freshly squeezed
lemon juice

5 ml/1 teaspoon
sugar syrup

chilled Champagne
or Crémant, to top

Serves 1

Unlikely as it sounds, this was named for the gun used by the French in World War I. It was a popular choice at Harry's New York Bar in Paris, so feel free, while you sip, to imagine yourself in the company of Hemingway and the Fitzgeralds…

Fill a cocktail shaker with ice cubes, add the gin, lemon juice and sugar syrup and shake well. Strain into a chilled Champagne flute. Top with Champagne and garnish with a long strip of lemon zest. Serve immediately.

CLOVER CLUB

This classic cocktail was first recorded in 1917. It consists of gin, lemon juice and raspberry syrup shaken with an egg white to give it a fluffy, foamy head. The addition of pink gin can only add to its enduring popularity!

INGREDIENTS

50 ml/1⅔ oz. pink gin

20 ml/¾ oz. freshly squeezed lemon juice

5 ml/1 teaspoon raspberry syrup (or Grenadine)

dash of very fresh egg white

sugar syrup, to taste

Serves 2

Add all the ingredients to a cocktail shaker filled with ice cubes and shake sharply. Strain into a cocktail coupe, garnish with a few raspberries (if using) and serve immediately.

BRAMBLE

Simple to make and well-balanced with sweet and sour notes, the bramble has become something of a modern classic.

Shake the gin, lemon juice and sugar syrup in a cocktail shaker with a good handful of ice cubes, then strain into a collins glass filled with crushed ice. Drizzle the crème de mûre over the ice and garnish with a lemon wedge and a fresh blackberry. Serve immediately.

INGREDIENTS

50 ml/1⅔ oz. gin

30 ml/1 oz. freshly squeezed lemon juice

10 ml/2 teaspoons sugar syrup

15 ml/½ oz. crème de mûre (blackberry liqueur)

Serves 2

GIN GIMLET

GLASSWARE

Wine glass

GARNISH

Cucumber batons

INGREDIENTS

50 ml/1⅔ oz. gin

25 ml/1 oz. lime cordial

Serves 2

'A popular beverage in the Navy', declared Harry McElhone in *Barflies and Cocktails*, no doubt because the sweet and scurvy-scotching lime made the gin ration more palatable. A simple and strengthening apéritif.

Fill a cocktail shaker with ice cubes and add the gin and lime cordial. Shake very well and strain into a chilled wine glass. Garnish with cucumber batons and serve immediately.

COCKTAIL BLEU

GLASSWARE

Martini glass

GARNISH

Orange zest

INGREDIENTS

35 ml/1¼ oz. gin

15 ml/½ oz. blue
Curaçao

15 ml/½ oz. Cointreau

5 ml/1 teaspoon freshly
squeezed lemon juice

5 ml/1 teaspoon sugar
syrup

Serves 2

The celebrated Parisian café La Coupole created a Cocktail Bleu in 1958 to celebrate 'Exposition du Vide', an exhibition by Yves Klein, artist and creator of the iconic colour International Klein Blue. This version is a twist on the classic White Lady.

Fill a cocktail shaker with ice cubes, add all the ingredients and shake well. Strain into a chilled martini glass, add a twist of orange zest, if using, and serve immediately.

ROSY GLOW

GLASSWARE

Champagne flute

GARNISH

Orange zest or
a peach slice

INGREDIENTS

30 ml/1 oz. peach-
flavoured gin

15 ml/½ oz. freshly
squeezed orange juice

15 ml/½ oz.
cranberry juice

well-chilled prosecco,
to top

Serves 1

Taking its lead from the classic 80s cocktail Sex on the Beach, this fruity sparkler replaces the traditional peach schnapps and vodka with a peach-flavoured gin with delicious results.

Put a Champagne flute in the fridge to chill. Pour the gin, orange juice and cranberry juice into an ice-filled cocktail shaker and shake well. Strain into the chilled flute and slowly top up with prosecco. Garnish with an orange zest or a peach slice and serve immediately.

JASMINE BLOSSOM

Coupe glass

**Jasmine leaves
or blossoms**

**35 ml/1¼ oz. freshly
brewed strong jasmine
tea, chilled**

**5 ml/1 teaspoon
orgeat syrup**

10 ml/2 teaspoons gin

**well-chilled Asti
Spumante or other
sparkling wine, to top**

Serves 1

The beautiful floral perfume of jasmine tea, given a little backbone by a dash of gin and the almond scent of orgeat, makes this an unusual but delightful daytime cocktail that will intrigue your guests.

Pour the jasmine tea, orgeat syrup and gin into an ice-filled cocktail shaker and shake well. Strain into a small coupe and top with Asti. Garnish with jasmine, if you like, and serve immediately.

25 ml/1 oz. gin

25 ml/1 oz. red vermouth

25 ml/1 oz. Campari

Serves 1

THE CLASSIC NEGRONI

An unbeatable cocktail – the perfect combination of three distinct ingredients in equal measures, that when mixed is better than the sum of its parts. Some people like to tinker with the proportions of gin, vermouth and Campari, but this equal parts Negroni is sublime in its simplicity...

Add the gin to an ice-filled glass, followed by the red vermouth and the Campari. Gently stir and garnish with an orange twist and serve immediately.

RASPBERRY
TOM COLLINS

This is a lovely, fruity twist on the Tom Collins. It was originally made with Old Tom, a slightly sweeter and smoother style of gin.

Fill a cocktail shaker with ice cubes and add all the ingredients except the soda water and raspberries. Shake well and stain into a highball glass filled with ice. Top up with soda water and stir, then garnish with lemon slices before serving immediately.

MARGUERITE

GLASSWARE

Coupe glass

GARNISH

Orange or pink
grapefruit zest

INGREDIENTS

35 ml/1¼ oz. gin

30 ml/1 oz. dry
vermouth

15 ml/½ oz. triple sec

dash of Angostura
bitters

Serves 1

This is a less well-known but extremely
soignée cousin of the Martini. It actually
preceded the Martini's invention, and
is utterly delicious.

Put a coupe glass in the fridge to chill. Fill
a cocktail shaker with ice cubes and add the
gin, vermouth, triple sec and Angostura bitters.
Stir well and strain into the chilled coupe glass.
Garnish with a twist of orange or pink grapefruit
zest and serve immediately.

THE JOURNALIST

Martini glass

Maraschino cherry

Equal parts dry and sweet vermouth, this drink is crisp, rich and complex. Originally appearing in the *Savoy Cocktail Book* in 1930, this drink is a sure fix for journalists and beyond.

25 ml/1 oz. gin

dash of sweet vermouth

dash of dry vermouth

2 dashes of freshly squeezed lemon juice

2 dashes of triple sec

2 dashes of Angostura bitters

Serves 1

Put a martini glass in the fridge to chill. Fill a cocktail shaker with ice cubes and add the gin, sweet vermouth, dry vermouth, lemon juice, triple sec and Angostura bitters. Stir well and strain into the chilled martini glass. Garnish with a maraschino cherry and serve immediately.

LAVENDER ROSÉ ROYALE

GLASSWARE

Coupe glass

GARNISH

Edible flowers

This gin-based delight is similar to a French 75 in style with the lavender giving it a subtle floral note.

INGREDIENTS

2 large strawberries, hulled

60 ml/2 oz. floral gin

15 ml/½ oz. freshly squeezed lemon juice

15 ml/½ oz. Monin lavender syrup

200 ml/¾–1 cup dry sparkling rosé, well chilled, to top

Serves 2

Put the strawberries into a cocktail shaker and muddle with a muddler or the end of a wooden rolling pin. Once pulped, add the gin, lemon juice, lavender syrup and 4–5 ice cubes. Shake until chilled, about 20 seconds. Strain the mixture into coupes, top up with the sparkling rosé and garnish with edible flowers. Serve immediately.

75 ml/2½ oz. pink gin

10 ml/2 teaspoons dry vermouth

Serves 2

PINK MARTINI

There are plenty of occasions that call for a fun, flirty pink drink, so here is a classic, reinvented with fruity pink gin.

Put a martini glass in the fridge to chill. Add all the ingredients to a cocktail shaker filled with ice cubes, shake sharply and strain into the chilled martini glass. Garnish with lemon zest and serve immediately.

KIWI MARTINI POPTAILS

GLASSWARE

Martini glass

INGREDIENTS

For the ice pops:

4 ripe kiwi fruits, peeled

100 ml/3½ oz. clear sparkling lemonade

1 tablespoon kiwi syrup

For the martinis:

240 ml/8 oz. gin

80 ml/2¾ oz. vermouth

4 tablespoons kiwi syrup

4 straight-sided silicone ice pop moulds

4 sticks

Serves 4

These vibrant green poptails, with a tangy refreshing sharpness from the kiwi, make a fun and stylish drink to serve to friends after dinner. When frozen, the kiwi seeds add a little crunch and the fruit takes on a sherbet tang. Kiwi syrup (such as the Monin brand) is available from online retailers and is worth investing in for these delicious poptails.

Prepare the ice pops first, as they need time to freeze. Cut one kiwi into four thick 1-cm/⅓-inch slices and set aside. Place the remaining three kiwis into the blender and blitz to a smooth purée. Add the lemonade and kiwi syrup and blitz again. Pour the mixture into the silicone moulds. Press a stick through the middle of a slice of kiwi and position the slice on top of the mixture with the stick upright. Repeat for the other sticks and moulds. Freeze for at least 8 hours or overnight until solid.

For the martinis, place the gin, vermouth and kiwi syrup into the cocktail shaker with ice and shake hard until chilled. Pour the martini through a strainer and divide into the glasses. Remove the ice pops from their moulds and place in the glasses. Serve immediately.

CHAISE LONGUE

25 ml/1 oz. gin

5 ml/1 teaspoon chilled absinthe

dash of rose water

125 ml/4¼ oz. well-chilled prosecco

Serves 1

This is based on a classic cocktail invented by Ernest Hemingway, Death in the Afternoon, but is tempered by the decidedly un-Hemingway-like addition of rose water. He would have added twice as much absinthe, but even as it is you might be glad of a lie down on a chaise longue after drinking one!

Pour the gin and absinthe into a chilled Champagne flute and add a dash of rose water. Gently pour over the prosecco, and then serve immediately.

ULTRA VIOLET

25 ml/1 oz. gin

20 ml/¾ oz. crème de violette

10 ml/2 teaspoons blue Curaçao

10 ml/2 teaspoons freshly squeezed lemon juice

well-chilled prosecco, to top

Serves 1

Roses are red, but violets are just so much more chic. Try out this subtly floral delight at your next drinks party and you'll be rewarded with plenty of oohs and aahs.

Put the gin, crème de violette, blue curaçao and lemon juice in a cocktail shaker and add a handful of ice cubes. Shake well, then strain into a chilled martini glass. Top with prosecco, garnish with lemon zest and serve immediately.

GLASSWARE

Martini glass

GARNISH

Lemon twist

CHELSEA SIDECAR

INGREDIENTS

45 ml/1¾ oz. dry gin

30 ml/1 oz. triple sec

30 ml/1 oz. freshly
squeezed lemon juice

5 ml/1 teaspoon sugar
syrup

Serves 2

Replace Cognac in a Sidecar with gin, and this is what you get! A joy once discovered when out of tonic at home but with triple sec to hand.

Shake all ingredients with an ice-filled shaker and strain into a small chilled martini glass. Garnish with a lemon twist and serve immediately.

AVIATION

GLASSWARE

Martini glass

GARNISH

Maraschino cherries

INGREDIENTS

50 ml/1⅔ oz. gin

**5 ml/1 teaspoon
Luxardo Maraschino**

**5 ml/1 teaspoon crème
de violette**

**25 ml/1 oz. freshly
squeezed lemon juice**

Serves 2

This beautiful violet cocktail dates from
the early 1900.

Add all the ingredients to a cocktail shaker full
of ice. Shake until frosted. Strain into small
martini glasses and garnish with a single
maraschino cherry. Serve immediately.

PARISIAN MARTINI

This simple but delicious apéritif showcases two of France's best-known liquors, vermouth and cassis, and is jazzed up here with a pink gin.

Put a martini glass in the fridge to chill. Fill a cocktail shaker with ice cubes and add the gin, vermouth and crème de cassis. Stir well and strain into the chilled martini glass. Garnish with a lemon zest and serve immediately.

SLOE GIN FIZZ

Live life in the sloe lane with this refreshing long drink, a combination of jammy sloe gin and soda.

Add all the ingredients, except the soda, to a cocktail shaker filled with ice cubes. Shake and strain into an ice-filled highball glass. Top up with soda water, garnish with lemon slices and serve immediately.

GIN FIZZ ROYALE

A decadent take on the Gin Fizz. Gin Fizzes were especially popular in the 1940s – so much so that some bars had to hire extra bartenders to handle all the shaking.

Fill a cocktail shaker with ice cubes and add the lemon juice, egg white, gin and sugar. Shake vigorously, then strain into a highball glass filled with ice. Top with Champagne and garnish with lemon slices. Serve immediately.

GLASSWARE
Highball glass

GARNISH
Lemon slices

INGREDIENTS

25 ml/1 oz. freshly squeezed lemon juice

1 egg white

50 ml/1⅔ oz. gin

1 teaspoon white sugar (or 15 ml/½ oz. sugar syrup)

Champagne, to top

Serves 2

WHITE NEGRONI

GLASSWARE

Rocks glass

GARNISH

Orange zest

INGREDIENTS

25 ml/1 oz. gin

25 ml/1 oz. Suze

25 ml/1 oz. Lillet Blanc

Serves 1

The white Negroni is typically less sweet than a red Negroni and has a strong, earthy bitterness with a light, almost marmalade, citrus lift to follow. The use of dry vermouth instead of Lillet makes the drink even dryer.

Add the ingredients to an ice-filled glass and gently stir. Garnish with an orange twist and serve immediately

PROSECCO WHITE LADY

35 ml/1¼ oz. gin

15 ml/½ oz. Cointreau

well-chilled prosecco, to top

15 ml/½ oz. freshly squeezed lemon juice

Serves 1

A cocktail legend made even lovelier, thanks to a generous helping of Prosecco. The White Lady is a slinky, sophisticated classic – and so will you be once you've sipped one of these!

Pour the gin and Cointreau into a cocktail shaker half-filled with ice cubes. Stir until very cold, then strain into a chilled martini glass. Top with prosecco and the lemon juice, and serve immediately.

PINK GIMLET

GLASSWARE

Martini glass

GARNISH

Lime zest

INGREDIENTS

75 ml/2½ oz. pale dry
rosé wine, well chilled

25 ml/1 oz. London
Dry Gin

25 ml/1 oz.
lime cordial

Serves 1

A classic drink is often one whose
beauty lies in its simplicity. This twist
on a gimlet, the crisp and reviving
aperitif, is a shameless treat for the
ever-growing number of gin devotees.

Pour the wine, gin and lime cordial into an ice-
filled cocktail shaker, stir with a bar spoon until
very cold then strain into a martini glass. Twist
the lime zest to release its citrus oil on top of the
drink. Garnish the rim of the glass with the zest
or simply float it on the surface of the drink.
Serve immediately.

GIN RICKEY

GLASSWARE

Highball glass

GARNISH

Lime zest

INGREDIENTS

60 ml/2 oz. London
Dry Gin

15 ml/½ oz. freshly
squeezed lime juice

8 ml/1½ teaspoons
sugar syrup (or to taste)

soda water, to top

Serves 2

The Gin Rickey will forever be associated
with F. Scott Fitzgerald, thanks to the
'four gin rickeys that clicked full of ice'
in *The Great Gatsby*. A regular in many
bars, Fitzgerald wrote in another novel,
The Beautiful and the Damned, 'Here's to
alcohol, the rose-colored glasses of life'.

Fill a cocktail shaker with ice cubes and add the
gin, lime juice and sugar syrup, if using. Shake
well and strain into an ice-filled highball glass.
Top up with soda water. Garnish with a long strip
of lime zest and serve immediately.

ROSIE LEA

GLASSWARE

Tea cups or tumblers

GARNISH

Lime slices

INGREDIENTS

120 ml/4 oz. gin

60 ml/2 oz. triple sec

320 ml/10¾ oz.
cranberry juice

freshly squeezed juice
of 1 lime

Serves 4

Is it a classy cocktail? A refreshing sweetened tea? Or a fun drink perfect for an afternoon tea party? Yes, yes and yes.

Add the gin, triple sec, cranberry and lime juices to a large clean teapot or a jug/pitcher filled with ice cubes. Stir well and pour into tea cups or tumblers, garnish each one with a slice of lime and serve immediately.

AVIATION ROYALE

25 ml/1 oz. gin

10 ml/2 teaspoons
freshly squeezed
lemon juice

8 ml/1½ teaspoons
Maraschino

dash of crème
de violette

well-chilled Champagne
or other dry sparkling
wine, to top

Serves 1

A sparkling variation on the classic Aviation. It's based on a sophisticated combination of gin and Maraschino, with a splash of crème de violette for its perfume.

Pour the first four ingredients into an ice-filled cocktail shaker and stir well. Strain into a chilled coupe glass and top with Champagne. Garnish with a maraschino cherry and serve immediately.

RAMOS GIN FIZZ

The classic Gin Fizz is very similar to the Tom Collins. This popular version, created in New Orleans in 1888, includes egg white and cream for a richer texture.

Fill a cocktail shaker with ice cubes and add all the ingredients. Shake vigorously for as long as you can, then shake some more. Strain the mixture into a chilled highball glass and garnish with a slice of lemon. Serve immediately.

50 ml/1⅔ oz. gin

**25 ml/1 oz. single/
light cream**

20 ml/¾ oz. egg white

**20 ml/¾ oz. freshly
squeezed lemon juice**

**20 ml/¾ oz. freshly
squeezed lime juice**

20 ml/¾ oz. sugar syrup

**2 dashes orange-
flower water**

soda water, to top

Serves 2

GLASSWARE

Highball glass

INGREDIENTS

500 g/8 cups watermelon chunks, with seeds removed

500 ml/2 cups watermelon-flavoured gin

125 ml/½ cup freshly squeezed lime juice

60 ml/2 oz. sugar syrup

250 ml/1 cup well-chilled Cava

Serves 14

WATERMELON GIN & LIME COOLER

This juicy watermelon and gin cooler is guaranteed to keep you cool even on the hottest of days.

Whizz up the watermelon pieces in a blender, then pass through a very fine sieve/strainer set over a large jug/pitcher. Discard any bits of seeds left in the sieve/strainer.

Stir in the gin, lime juice, sugar syrup and Cava. Half-fill high ball glasses with crushed ice and pour in the cocktail to fill. Serve immediately.

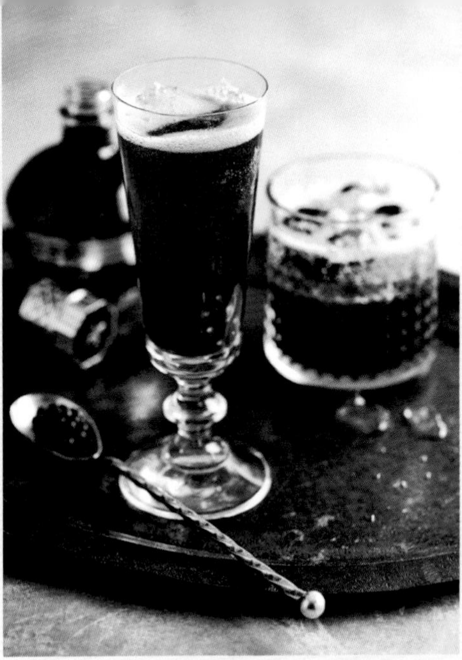

BLACKBERRY BARFLY

Dark and heady, with a deliciously unexpected tang of balsamic vinegar, this is a perfect late-night reviver.

GLASSWARE

Champagne flute

INGREDIENTS

5 blackberries

½ teaspoon balsamic vinegar

25 ml/1 oz. sloe gin

well-chilled prosecco, to top

Serves 1

Put the blackberries in a cocktail shaker with the balsamic vinegar and crush with a muddler until they release all their juice. Add the sloe gin and a handful of crushed ice and shake well. Strain into a Champagne flute and top with prosecco. Serve immediately.

GIN & TONIC ICE POPS

The gin and tonic has become a very popular choice of drink. These ice pops give gin a new spin, and are perfectly refreshing for a hot day.

INGREDIENTS

**4 thin slices
of cucumber**

**4 thin slices of lemon,
preserved in
lemon juice**

**350 ml/12 oz.
tonic water**

**freshly squeezed juice
of 1 lemon or 1 lime**

50 ml/1⅔ oz. gin

**4 ice pop moulds
4 sticks**

Serves 4

Place a cucumber slice and a lemon slice in each ice pop mould, with room between to fill with the liquid. (If you prefer you can just use cucumber or lemon rather than both, it is up to you.)

Mix the tonic water, lemon or lime juice and gin together in a jug/pitcher and pour into the moulds. Add the sticks in a straight, upright position. Freeze for at least 8 hours or overnight until they are solid.

When ready to serve, remove the gin and tonic ice pops from their moulds and serve immediately.

KITCHEN SINK NEGRONI

This could be described as the Long Island Iced Tea of the Negroni world. It contains a variety of ingredients, each contributing to its flavour profile: the dry gin adds a botanical intensity, Campari adds its unique bittersweetness and the Pimms adds complexity.

Combine the ingredients in a highball glass and stir. Add ice and top up with chilled tonic water. Garnish with a generous lemon peel and serve immediately.

NIGHT OWL

GLASSWARE

Martini glass

GARNISH

Lemon zest

INGREDIENTS

15 ml/½ oz. gin

15 ml/½ oz. crème
de cassis

15 ml/½ oz.
pomegranate juice

well-chilled prosecco,
to top

Serves 1

Any night owl worth their salt, and even a few who should know better, will enjoy this wickedly quaffable creation.

Put the gin, cassis and pomegranate juice in a cocktail shaker with a handful of ice cubes and shake well. Strain into a chilled martini glass and top with prosecco. Squeeze the lemon zest strip in half lengthways so that the essential oils in the skin spritz on to the drink, then drop it in. Serve immediately.

BERETTA 18

GLASSWARE

Champagne flute

GARNISH

Lemon zest

INGREDIENTS

25 ml/1 oz. gin

15 ml/½ oz. limoncello

well-chilled prosecco,
to top

Serves 1

Another Italian take on a classic, the French 75. Both are named after World War I artillery and both are classy numbers – serve up one of these and you're bound to impress your guests.

Put the gin and limoncello in a cocktail shaker or collins glass with a handful of ice cubes and stir until they are very cold. Strain into a chilled Champagne flute and top with prosecco. Squeeze the lemon zest in half lengthways over the drink so that the essential oils in the skin spritz over it, then drop it in and serve immediately.

COCOMANGO

GLASSWARE

Champagne flute

GARNISH

Dried mango strip

INGREDIENTS

15 ml/½ oz. coconut rum

15 ml/½ oz. gin

25 ml/1 oz. mango juice

10 ml/2 teaspoons freshly squeezed lime juice

dash of Angostura bitters (optional)

well-chilled Asti Spumante or other sparkling wine, to top

Serves 1

This delicous taste of the tropics is a lighter and more quaffable alternative to heavy coconut-based, tiki-style drinks.

Pour the first five ingredients into an ice-filled cocktail shaker and shake well. Strain into a chilled Champagne flute and top with Asti Spumante. Garnish with a strip of dried mango, if you like, and serve immediately.

TIKI NEGRONI

GLASSWARE

Rocks glass

GARNISH

Lime wheel, small
pineapple wedge,
pineapple leaves

INGREDIENTS

25 ml/1 oz. gin

25 ml/1 oz. red
vermouth

25 ml/1 oz. Campari

25 ml/1 oz. rum
(pineapple flavoured,
if you can find it)

3–4 dashes Angostura
Bitters

Serves 1

Picking up on the tiki trend, gin and rum are combined here to create a drink full of plump tropical notes with a balanced sweetness. The key to this recipe is the pineapple rum, a delicacy in Victorian England and the preferred drink of the Dickens' character Reverend Stiggins in *The Pickwick Papers*. The pineapple has long been a symbol of hospitality; look at the lid on Tanqueray Gin and you'll see a pineapple.

Add the ingredients to an ice-filled cocktail shaker and shake vigorously. Fine-strain into an ice-filled rocks glass and garnish with a lime wheel, lime, pineapple wedge and leaves and serve immediately.

BRONX

GLASSWARE

Martini glass

GARNISH

Orange zest

INGREDIENTS

50 ml/1⅔ oz. gin

**20 ml/¾ freshly
squeezed
orange juice**

**a dash of sweet
vermouth**

a dash of dry vermouth

Serves 2

Created at the Waldorf Astoria in New York by head bartender Johnnie Salon.

Put a martini glass in the fridge to chill. Fill a cocktail shaker with ice cubes and add the gin, orange juice, sweet vermouth, and dry vermouth. Stir well and strain into the chilled martini glass. Garnish with orange zest and serve immediately.

ICED G & TEA

GLASSWARE

Highball glass

GARNISH

Lemon slices

INGREDIENTS

1 Earl Grey tea bag

1 tablespoon caster/
superfine sugar

30 ml/1 oz. gin

1 teaspoon freshly
squeezed lemon juice

dash of elderflower
cordial

well-chilled prosecco,
to top

Serves 1

Tea, gin and Prosecco: all your favourite refreshments in one glass! Heaven. Next time you fancy a Long Island Iced Tea, think again, and try this far more elegant cocktail instead.

Put the tea bag and sugar in a small heatproof jug/pitcher and pouring over 75 ml/2½ oz. boiling water, then leave for 5 minutes. Remove the tea bag and leave to cool to room temperature. Pour the cooled Earl Grey infusion into a highball glass and add the gin, lemon juice and elderflower cordial. Half-fill with ice cubes and stir well. Slowly top up with prosecco and garnish with a couple of lemon slices.
Serve immediately

NEGRONI FLOAT

A grown-up version of a drink that's been popular in ice cream parlours and soda fountains for decades. This surprising Negroni variation is indulgent, fun and delicious. The cola helps to lengthen the drink with additional botanical flavour and the creaminess of the ice cream complements the bittersweet flavour of the Campari.

Half fill a large, tall glass with ice and add the gin, Campari, red vermouth and ice cream before carefully (and slowly) topping up with chilled cola. Garnish with whipped cream, sprinkles and a fresh cherry. Serve with a straw, immediately.

GLASSWARE

Highball glass

GARNISH

Whipped cream, sprinkles, a fresh cherry

INGREDIENTS

15 ml/½ oz. gin

15 ml/½ oz. Campari

15 ml/½ oz. red vermouth

1 scoop vanilla ice cream

100 ml/3⅓ oz. cola

Serves 1

BABYCAKES

GLASSWARE

Champagne flute

GARNISH

Edible rose petals

INGREDIENTS

60 ml/2 oz. pink gin

20 ml/¾ oz. Chambord

5 ml/1 teaspoon rosewater

well-chilled Asti Spumante or other sparkling wine, to top

Serves 2

Look no further for the ultimate Valentine's sparkling cocktail. Red Berries, rosewater and a pink gin are just meant to be together.

Put two flutes in the fridge to chill. Pour the gin, Chambord and rosewater into an ice-filled cocktail shaker and stir well. Strain into the chilled flutes and slowly top up with the Asti Spumante. Garnish with rose petals and serve immediately.

BREAKFAST IN MILAN

OK, so you don't have to wake up in Milan, but you'll definitely feel a lot more chic after getting one of these down you, along with a melt-in-the-mouth pastry. Continental breakfast in bed, anyone?

Put the marmalade in a cocktail shaker with the lime juice, Campari, if using, and gin. Half-fill the shaker with ice cubes and shake vigorously. Strain into a cold martini glass and top with prosecco. Serve immediately.

MERMAID'S KISS

GLASSWARE

Tumbler

GARNISH

Lemon slices

INGREDIENTS

60 ml/2 oz. pink gin

30 ml/1 oz. hibiscus syrup, such as Monin

10 ml/2 teaspoons freshly squeezed lemon juice

well-chilled clear sparkling lemonade, to top

Serves 2

Make a splash and serve this fragrant and fun summer cocktail at your next pool party.

Half-fill a tumbler with ice cubes. Add the gin, hibiscus syrup and lemon juice. Top up with chilled lemonade and stir gently before serving immediately with paper straws and lemon slices.

THE EARL

GLASSWARE

Balloon glass

GARNISH

Orange zest

INGREDIENTS

50 ml/1⅔ oz. gin

1 Earl Grey tea bag

150 ml/5 oz. tonic water

Serves 2

Tea is a great accompaniment to gin and it is quick and easy to infuse. Earl Grey has rich aromas, and also a zesty flair from the bergamot.

Add the gin to a glass and add the tea bag; allow to infuse for 60 seconds before using the mixture. Add fresh ice cubes to fill ¾ of the glass. Stir gently for 15 seconds with a bar spoon to chill the glass. Pour away any liquid from the melted ice. Top up the glass with more ice. Add the tea-infused gin, trying to ensure that you coat the ice as you pour. Add the tonic water. Pouring slowly helps the tonic to keep its fizz. Add the orange zest to the glasses. Let rest for 30 seconds to allow the flavours to integrate with each other, and serve immediately.

GLASSWARE

Wine glass

GARNISH

Edible rose petals

INGREDIENTS

75 ml/2½ oz. pink gin

1 x 750-ml/25-oz. bottle
chilled pale rosé wine

250 ml/1 cup
elderflower cordial

125 ml/½ cup freshly
squeezed lemon juice

30 ml/1 oz. rosewater

1–1½ litres/4–6 cups
chilled tonic water

cucumber slices

lemon slices

Serves 6–8

THE PINK & THE GREEN

**A fragrant and delicate summer cup that
perfectly showcases a pink gin.**

Pour the gin, wine, elderflower cordial, lemon
juice and rosewater into a large punch bowl.
Add plenty of ice cubes to chill, then add tonic
to taste. Follow with the cucumber and lemon
and stir. Scatter over the rose petals just before
serving, if using. Ladle into ice cube-filled wine
glasses, adding a little of the fruit and edible rose
petals to each glass (if using). Serve immediately.

GOLDFISH BOWL

GLASSWARE

Balloon glass

GARNISH

Fish-shaped gummy candy and rosemary sprigs

INGREDIENTS

50 ml/1⅔ oz. gin

10 ml/2 teaspoons blue Curaçao

150 ml/5 oz. bitter lemon tonic

50 ml/1⅔ oz. lemonade

Serves 2

This drink is inspired by the nickname of the copita glass: 'goldfish bowl'. It is made using a bright and zesty gin from Sweden, paired with a combination of lemon tonic and lemonade, plus a splash of blue Curaçao.

Add fresh ice cubes to fill ¾ of the glass. Stir gently for 15 seconds with a bar spoon to chill the glass. Pour away any liquid from the melted ice. Top up the glass with more ice. Add the gin, trying to ensure that you coat the ice as you pour. Add the blue Curaçao, tonic water and lemonade. Pouring slowly helps the tonic to keep its fizz. Add the gummy candy and rosemary. Let rest for 30 seconds to allow the flavours to integrate with each other and serve immediately.

CHOCOLATE GIN TONICA

The dark (bittersweet) chocolate notes of the bitters finish this drink off nicely, bringing the flavours together, adding depth and creating the perfect drink for Valentine's Day.

GLASSWARE

Balloon glass

GARNISH

Chocolate or sugar syrup, chocolate flakes and chopped pistachios

INGREDIENTS

50 ml/1⅔ oz. gin (chocolate flavoured, if you can find it)

200 ml/6¾ oz. tonic water

3–4 dashes of cocoa bitters

Serves 2

First prepare the glass by dipping the rim in chocolate or sugar syrup and then into a saucer of chocolate flakes. Add fresh ice cubes to fill ¾ of the glass. Stir gently for 15 seconds with a bar spoon to chill the glass. Pour away any liquid from the melted ice. Top up the glass with more ice. Add the gin, trying to ensure that you coat the ice as you pour. Add the tonic water and cocoa bitters. Pouring slowly helps the tonic to keep its fizz. Add the syrup, chocolate flakes and chopped pistachios. Let it rest for 30 seconds to allow the flavours to integrate with each other and then serve immediately.

RECIPE CREDITS

Julia Charles:
Aviation
Bramble
Chelsea Sidecar
Clover Club
Lavender Rosé Royale
Mermaid's Kiss
Pink Gimlet
Pink Martini
Rosie Lea
The Pink & The Green
Watermelon Gin & Lime
  Cooler

Laura Gladwin:
Aviation Royale
Babycakes
Beretta 18
Blackberry Barfly
Breakfast in Milan
Chaise Longue
Cocktail Bleu
CocoMango
French 75
Iced G & Tea

Jasmine Blossom
La Passeggiata
Mango Morning
Marguerite
Night Owl
Parisian Martini
Prosecco White Lady
Rosy Glow
Sapphire
Sloe Gin Fizz
Ultra Violet

Hannah Miles:
Gin & Tonic Ice Pops
Kiwi Martini Poptails

Lottie Muir:
Field of Dreams

Ben Reed:
Bronx
Gin Fizz Royale
Gin Gimlet
Gin Rickey
Raspberry Tom Collins
Sapphire
The Journalist

David T. Smith & Keli Rivers:
Classic Negroni
Kitchen Sink Negroni
Negroni Float
Tiki Negroni
White Negroni

David T. Smith:
Chocolate Gin Tonica
Goldfish Bowl
The Earl

Tristan Stephenson:
Ramos Gin Fizz

William Yeoward's American Bar:
Gin Sling
White Lady

PICTURE CREDITS

Laura Edwards:
Page 44

Georgia Glynn-Smith:
Page 62

Gavin Kingcome:
Pages 8, 10

Adrian Lawrence:
Pages 19, 34

William Lingwood:
Pages 9, 23, 35, 36

Alex Luck:
Pages 6, 7, 12-14, 20-22,
26, 29-33, 37-39, 43, 46,
47-51, 53, 56-58, 60,
61-63

Gareth Morgans
Pages 15, 17, 27, 41, 59

David Vessey:
Page 18

Clare Winfield:
Page 11